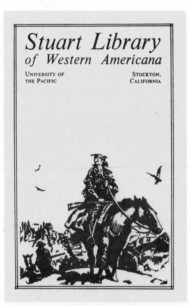

TO ALASKA FOR GOLD

THE John F. Stacey booklet on gold mining in the Klondike is a mildly rare item presumably printed in Massachusetts in 1916. The original unhelpfully carries no date or place of printing. It is rather probable that descendents of John F. Stacey are living in New Hampshire or Massachusetts at this time but considerable searching failed to locate any. The original title page states that the author lived in So. Ashburton, Massachusetts. The booklet was dictated to his daughter, Mrs. John A. Davis, of Worcester, Massachusetts. These pages, crudely printed more than half a century ago, tell an old story that amateurs in search of gold often gain more experience than precious metal.

Of this booklet three hundred copies were printed.

This is copy Number **68**.

TO

FOR

GOLD

JOHN F. STACEY

YE GALLEON PRESS

Fairfield, Washington

1973

Library of Congress Cataloging in Publication Data

Stacey, John F

    To Alaska for Gold.

       Edition limited to 300 copies; this is no.

       Reprint of the ed. originally published about 1916.

       1. Stacey, John F.   2. Klondike gold fields.

I. Title.

F931.S785 1973   917.12'1   73-7598
ISBN 0-87770-096-6

ISBN 0-87770-096-6

TABLE OF CONTENTS

THE MOULTON KLONDIKE COMPANY

INTRODUCTION

Often in the years since I followed the feverish crowd I have heard the question, "Why don't you write the whole story?" Friends have assured me my experiences were of sufficient interest, and finally because of my desire to show to people conditions as they were at that time I have been persuaded to set down this simple account of just what I did and saw and experienced during the months I was away from home.

As I recall those days they seem but yesterday and so vivid is each incident in my memory that I think I have not fallen short of my aim, which was an absolutely truthful account of my experiences. I trust it may be of interest to others.

JOHN F. STACEY.

CHAPTER I.

The Start.

When a friend of mine came to me and said, "Why don't you go to Alaska?" I said I thought I was too old to take such a trip. (I was fifty-three at that time.) He seemed to think I could outdo the young men yet. When I talked it over with my wife she said, as I might have known she would, "If you really want to go I will try and get along some way, for I don't want to put anything in your way."

This was in 1896 and the papers were full of all sorts of stories of Alaska and the wonderful riches of that new country. Among other things about this time we ran across an advertisement stating that the Moulton Klondike Mining Co. of Manchester, N. H. wanted more members for a party then forming to go to the Klondike. I wrote them about taking both my friend and myself as members of their party. We arranged to meet in Boston at a nearby date to talk the matter over. At this meeting they invited us to go to Manchester to meet the whole party.

As it turned out I took the trip to Manchester alone, as my friend was obliged to give up all thought of the matter because of conditions at home. At this meeting I was accepted as a member of the Moulton Klondike Mining Company and we voted not to take any more

11

members, as the party now numbered twelve. Our company was incorporated under the laws of Maine. We voted that each member should pay into the treasury the sum of one thousand dollars, five hundred payable the first of January 1897, the other five hundred the first of March.

The steamship company which was to take us from Seattle notified us to be at that port about the tenth of May, as we would probably sail from there around the twentieth. While we were making preparations for being there the tenth of May we got word from the steamship company that they wanted us there the tenth of April because they had found a new route where they could keep on a southern coast and get through to St. Michael earlier in the season; so we hastened our preparations, bade our loved ones farewell, and after five days on the train arrived at Seattle in time to sail on the twentieth of April.

I speak advisedly when I say we arrived "in time to sail," for we did not sail. There was no boat there to take us. They said they expected the Bricksum and the Laurador any day. We heard this same report every day while we waited.

While we were waiting we stayed at the Globe Hotel and took our meals wherever we happened to be. The hotel was only a few rods from what they called the "dead line," below which there were no police and one going there took his life in his hands. One man from Gardner was drinking in a roadhouse one night and when he came to the next day he found himself away down below the dead line with all his money gone. The place was full of crooks of all kinds. Neither the proprietor of the road house nor the police would help him any so he had to send home for some money.

The Salvation Army used to play on the wharf three times a week and I went down to hear them one night. A big fellow came along and asked me to go down and see a string of cars which were loaded with parts of river boats to be shipped to the Yukon. After going a little way I thought it was time to turn back and said I had seen enough, but he wanted me to go further. I always felt he wanted to get me down there where he could take what I had.

There was another man who wanted our party to go over the trail from Juno and beat the boat to Dawson. In that way he said we should get our choice of claims to stake. But we decided to stick to our original plans and go by boat. It was a good thing we did for we discovered afterward that he was a crook.

The Bricksum sailed first, but not until about the twentieth of May. We waited for the Laurador which came in three days later. Three hundred and ninety-six miners had tickets to sail on this boat, so the company loaded the freight as fast as possible in order to start at once.

When almost ready to sail we discovered that five of the staterooms had no outside ventilation. We entered a complaint asking that some windows be cut, but our request was refused.

About this time six men worked a day and a half loading on boxes which looked like the boxes used for shipping friut. We were notified we were to sail within a day or two, going by the way of Vancouver. Then three official looking men came to inspect the boat before she started. They thought those boxes looked suspicious and they opened one of them. It proved to be full of liquor, which being unlawful to transport from the States to Alaska they of course ordered unloaded. Another day and a half and the boxes were on shore again and we were again notified that the boat was to sail, but this time to Vancouver to take on a cargo of liquor for

13

Dawson. This liquor being sealed and going from one Canadian port to another they were allowed to carry. If we wished to stay on board and make this trip to Vancouver and back we could do so free of charge.

ON THE ROCKS

CHAPTER II.

Adventures by the Way.

We went to Vancouver, took on our cargo, and started back for Seattle the same night, but late in the evening while our captian and pilot seemed to be having a jolly good time in the cabin with some friends, we ran up on the shore.

I was in my berth when it happened but it went up on the ground so slowly I knew no great harm was done, or at least that we were in no immediate danger. But I went up on deck and found people in quite a panic. There was one big fat man weighing about three hundred and fifty pounds who was running around screaming and scaring everybody by his actions. One life preserver would not go around him so he had managed to tie two of them together and get them about his waist. The captain gave him a choice string of oaths when he saw him and told him to stop scaring the women and children as there was no danger.

I saw that what he said was true and so went back to my berth. The berth I occupied was built crosswise of the ship and when I lay down I was level but when I woke up my head was considerably lower than my feet so I had to change about end for end. The tide had gone out since we struck and laid the boat over on its side.

16

There was nothing for us to do but stay there till morning. Daylight brought many tugs large and small to bid for the job of towing us off, and one big tug came up along side and someone on board called out, "Want some help?"

"Yes," answered our captain.

"How much will you give to be towed off?"

"Fifty dollars," was the answer.

"One hundred dollars and we will do it."

"Too much," called the captain. However he finally agreed to pay the hundred dollars for the job.

This tug had a sort of light railing around the deck and the tow line was hitched near the middle of the tug. I don't know what went wrong but when the tug's engine started she began to spin around and around taking off the railing as clean as could be and making all the men on her deck jump rope pretty lively. Of course we all welcomed this ridiculous spectacle as a pleasant break in the monotony of waiting, but after pulling for fifteen or twenty minutes with no apparent result the tug got enough of us and gave up the job and the one hundred dollars. That she gave up so soon she must have regretted, for in a few minutes after she left us we very quietly moved out from the shore. The many pulls the tug gave us very likely loosened us somewhat from our position, and combined with a rise in the tide left us free to go on our way.

We thought that was all there was to that adventure but when we reached Seattle we learned some more about it. Vancouver is on an island and it seemed its water was carried from the mainland through pipes under the channel. When we ran up on shore we cut their water pipes and left Vancouver without water. The officers came to seize the ship but arrived about twenty minutes after we had sailed away. Had they been in time to take the ship we very likely should never have gone to Alaska.

Now comes a strange thing. When we again reached Seattle the portholes we had requested were cut in our staterooms and the very same boxes of liquor were loaded on again. Then the very same three officers who had previously ordered them off came aboard looking very important and again inspected the cargo, and this time declared everything all right and signed the ship's clearance papers. In some way their eyes seemed to have been blinded since the last inspection.

CHAPTER III.

From Seattle to Dutch Harbor.

Finally on the thirteenth of June we really started on our way, going through the six hundred mile inner passage where we enjoyed the most beautiful scenery I had ever seen, spending a night in a quiet bay while a violent, storm raged outside, and then passing out into a rough sea and later a fog so dense we could not see across the deck. We supposed the captain knew where we were going and felt no special uneasiness as day after day passed and we still saw only fog, until one day an old whaler who was among the passengers said, "Do you think you are headed for Dutch Harbor? Well you are not, you are headed straight for Siberia."

"How do you know?" we asked him.

"I haven't traveled these seas all my life for nothing," was the reply.

"Why don't you tell the captain?"

"He snubbed me once and he isn't going to get a chance to do it again."

Well, we were in the fog for eleven days and when we came out of it we were, as the old whaler had said, headed about as straight for Siberia as one could be, and had to change our course about ninety degrees to turn toward Dutch Harbor. We had been all this time off the beaten tracks of

the sea and not having been seen by any other
steamer had been reported lost at sea. So when
we steamed into Dutch Harbor they were some
surprised to see us.

We had expected to find the Bricksum at
Dutch Harbor but having taken so much longer
than we should have to make the port we
learned she had made Dutch Harbor, had
returned to Seattle for more freight, landed
at Dutch Harbor a second time and now
had gone on to St. Michael. In making this
second trip back to Seattle before going to St.
Michael she had caused some of the travelers on
board much inconvenience. When she arrived at
Dutch Harbor the first time all the passengers on
board had been informed that they must take off
all their baggage and live on shore while the
Bricksum went back to Seattle for another load
of freight. The contract the company had signed
with these men was that they would carry them
through to St. Michael, so the men of course felt
they were not being used fairly. In hope of
justice they called on the revenue cutter Bear
which was patrolling Bering Sea and the Pacific
Ocean and was supposed to look after the rights
of American citizens. But these officers had no
hesitation in saying that the men must go ashore
as they had been told. There was no appeal,
the men were helpless and they had to put up
their tents on shore and live on their own
provisions for six weeks while the Bricksum
made another trip to Seattle and back. All
this time they of course could do nothing
for their own benefit and it seemed very
unfair that they should have to live on their own
food when the company had not yet carried out
its part of the contract. However as I said there
was no appeal in such cases and the men had to
stand the loss. At the end of the six weeks the
Bricksum returned with more freight, took on

her passengers and went to St. Michael. It was just after she had left this second time that we arrived at Dutch Harbor.

CHAPTER IV.

Dutch Harbor.

Perhaps if you could see this trading post or small village you would have been as surprised as I was. Dutch Harbor and Unalaska are both on the coast, one on each side of a hill running out perpendicularly to the shore. They both had docks at which steamers called about once in three weeks. Each place had a store whose proprietors had been there for years, but most of the rest of the population were natives with the exception of the travelers who were merely going through.

As we were waiting here eight or nine days I got pretty well acquainted with the place and the people. Back from Unalaska lay a large strip of the most beautiful rolling country I had ever seen. There were mountains on both sides, but in between it seemed to me there must be as much as two thousand acres of such land as reminded me of the land I had seen in Minnesota. All growth was luxuriant and many kinds of flowers grew wild in profusion. It seemed to me it would be a grand place for farming and I said as much to the storekeeper at Unalaska one day. They told me the climate never varied more than ten degrees between summer and winter, hardly ever freezing and I thought it would be ideal for year around farming.

But he said, "No, it has been tried, but it is too wet. All the year around it rains some every day. Not much perhaps, but some, and this keeps the ground wet all the time. They have tried to drain it but it is so level it could not be done, so they had to give it up."

"I should think it would be a fine grazing country," I said.

"No, that has been tried too but the cattle all died from hoof rot. I have two cows and I never have to cut any hay. But I can only turn them out for an hour or so and then put them on the dry floor where their feet can dry out again. A while ago the government put twenty-nine reindeer here but there is only one left now. They all died with the hoof rot."

I sometimes watched the boats unloading at the docks and one day a pilot came in so fast he smashed off twenty-seven piles right near where I was standing but I managed to jump to safety. I was told each pile would cost one hundred dollars to replace. Another day we watched a couple who had gone out in a small row boat. They got into the undertow around the point between the two towns and had to be rescued. They could never have gotten out of it alone.

CHAPTER V.

Dutch Harbor to St. Michael.

At Dutch Harbor we took on more passengers who were waiting for us. We also had to tow two river boats which the company had been building at Dutch Harbor for use on the Yukon River and these too were loaded with freight.

With this heavy load we again went on, stopping at Sitka for three days. There the officers of the steamship company came on board and we thought it a good time to enter another complaint. So far on our voyage we had had miserable food cooked by Chinese cooks. We now asked or rather demanded that these cooks as well as the purser who had also been very mean in many ways should be discharged. They could see no way of getting rid of the cooks as there was no one else on board who could take their places. As for the purser they did discharge him but he certainly had the best of us then, for he took the rest of the trip as a gentleman of leisure and smiled at us complacently.

Some of us who wished to went on shore here after getting a permit, but we did not see very much of the place this time. We did enjoy the trip into the harbor though. The way winds in and out through a thousand islands taking so intricate a course that no captain tried to go in nearer than forty miles without a pilot. There were two pilots in the city who had towers from which they could see boats at sea and know when their services were needed. The pilot who answered our signal came out that forty miles in a small row boat rowed by four men and arrived in a few hours.

After leaving Sitka we now thought our next port would surely be St. Michael but after going nearly two hundred miles there was a call of distress from one of the river boats behind, and as the captain could not get much information from their signals he decided to send back a small boat to investigate. This lowering of the small boat in so rough a sea was a very interesting process for us landsmen. The boat was made ready, the men in place and it was lowered till it almost touched the water. We wondered how they were ever going to do it. But the mate began to count.

"One, two, three, no I'm wrong," he shouted.

And again he counted, "One, two, three, four, five, six, seven, go!"

At the word "go" the boat was dropped and it shot away from the steamer's side as though it were sent by a cannon. The mate explained to us that the eighth wave always takes the boat away safely.

The trouble with the river boat proved to be a bad leak which would necessitate a return to Sitka for repairs before we could proceed to St. Michael. It was just after dinner when the mate undertook to turn us around for our return. Having the river boats dragging us back made turning very difficult and as we came around we got into the trough of the sea, immediately dropped down what seemed to me like about forty feet, way down between two waves. For an instant we stayed there, then as the waves came together we were heaved up like a mere eggshell. I was standing on the upper deck and braced myself between the house and the rail but felt a very strange sensation from the motion.

Paul Parkhurst, the youngest man of our party, stood on this deck also and near him was a barrel of sperm oil held to the deck by ropes around the barrel. As the boat lifted, this barrel was lifted from its mooring and the oil spilled all over the deck. Paul who had nothing to get hold of slid across the deck in the oil and had he not been quick enough to throw up his hands and catch the rail as he went under he would have been swept off the deck with nobody but me to see him go.

Down in the dining room things were happening too. The tables which had not been cleared since dinner were now cleared with a mighty crash and there were so few dishes that were not broken that the stewards gathered up the whole mess; dishes, food, silver and all, and threw it into the sea.

With no more mishaps we made our return to Sitka and stayed there for a week. Of course we had to be examined by the health officers again although we had left there only a short time before. As for me I was quite anxious to get on shore to get something to eat, for I had not felt very much like eating for sometime, and now that the motion of the boat had stopped I began to feel hungry. So I suggested to three others of the party that we go to a restaurant and see what we could get to eat. We easily found an eating place and the proprietor wanted to know what we wanted. I told him a whole pan full of onions and potatoes fried together. We waited while he prepared these and it didn't take us long to get rid of them, and then another pan full which we ordered and waited for.

Now feeling better we started out to see the city, and before the week was over we had done this pretty well. We got acquainted with several

27

of the government officers, and one whom we knew especially well we told about the boxes of liquor which had been put on the second time at Seattle. He was interested and said he would go to St. Michael with us.

When we arrived at St. Michael we were told we had to unload our own provisions. This meant that we with the other parties on board had to unload the whole eight hundred tons of provisions in order to get our own twenty tons, for it was so mixed together in the hold that we could not get all of ours till the whole was unloaded. In fact the last thing taken out was a bag of beans belonging to our party. Even the liquor was so mixed up with the provisions that we had to take it all out. As fast as it was unloaded the officer who had come up from Sitka with us seized it. However as soon as the boat was unloaded they began loading it on again and when questioned about it the officer said it was the governor's orders. The governor lived a thousand miles away and the last we knew was not at home, but of course they might have received a telegram from him as they said. But whoever gave the orders it was illegal transportation of liquor.

CHAPTER VI.

Up the River to Rampart City.

Those who were not going up the river put their goods in storehouses but we loaded ours directly on to the river boats and the barge, which was only another boat like the one we traveled on with the exception that it had no steam and had to be towed by the boat.

Without much delay the river boat made ready to start. We started, but that was all. We had not been moving five minutes when our boat struck a rock which made a hole in the bottom and sent us rushing for shore. It was found that the hole was right under where our goods were piled, so once more we had the pleasure of handling our twenty tons; this time on planks we carried it to the shore and stacked it up while the repairs were made. Divers mended the hole under water and it took only a few days, after which we put our stuff all back in place again and made another start.

We were not allowed to get out of the habit of working on this trip up the Yukon. When we started they told us they had coal enough to take us three hundred miles and that after that we should get up steam by wood which they had ready cut and stacked on the shore all the way up.

The tide is felt for two hundred miles up the river and up another hundred miles are some

rapids which we were able to make only by
tacking ship and gaining a little each turn. By
the time we had passed these our coal was all
gone and there was no wood to be seen. Their
wood cutting must have been done in their
imaginations for we found no traces of any on
the rest of the trip and the only way we were
able to go on was for the passengers to get out
and cut wood as it was needed on the rest of the
way, which proved to be about seven hundred
miles. We had to go out into the woods, cut the
wood and bring it to the shore and load it on
the boat.

Occasionally we saw native homes on the way
up the river. Some were made of snow and some
of dirt, but all of the same shape, rounded up
like a haystack and with a hole in the front big
enough for a person to crawl in on hands and
knees. We saw one of these one day just as a
big, fat woman, with short skirts was going to
crawl in. A man on board had a camera and
snapped a picture of her, but would not give any
of us one of the pictures.

The lack of wood was not the only diffculty.
In the Yukon we found floating sandbars. No
matter how well a pilot might know the bottom
of the river one day, he might find it different
the next day, for one of these sandbars might be
found in one place one day and it might be moved
to a new place the next day. We got on several
of these during the trip and had a rather hard
time getting off. The river is very shallow in
some places anyway so that the river boats only
carry three feet of water when they are loaded,
but even so we got stuck pretty often and finally
got on one from which we had to be towed by
another river boat. This boat towed us right
into Rampart City, and on the morning of the
first day of September I awoke to find myself in
port.

As it was getting so late in the season we feared we should not be able to reach Dawson as we had planned before the river should freeze, so after talking the matter over we decided to unload our goods and stop at Rampart City.

CHAPTER VII.

A Month of Hard Work.

Now came the immediate need of a place to stay before night, as well as a location and materials for a permanent home. This was to mean over a month of such work as few builders under normal conditions know anything about.

Moulton, our president, and Garlick, treasurer, started off to find a good location to build, leaving me to look after putting up the two tents for that night. I had one all put up and another partly up when they returned to say they had found a suitable place for us on a knoll right beside the river, so we took our tents there and set them up again. We named the place Knob Hill. Our tents were placed close together with the space between covered on top and on the back so that we could use this place for cooking. One of the tents was to hold our provisions and the other was our sleeping quarters.

That night we left two men with our supplies on the shore and next morning saw us hard at work bringing them up to our new home. Each man had three hundred pounds of personal equipment besides the twenty tons of provisions and it was no small or easy task to bring these all up the hill about a third of a mile in our hands or on our backs whichever way best suited us. It gave us two days of hard tugging to get them all safely housed in our tent.

Then the whole attention was turned to looking for logs to build our permanent home. Rampart City had been settled too long for us to find wood nearby, for it had been all cut for previous housebuilders; and we found we had to travel four miles up the Yukon, then another mile up the Big Minook, a tributary of the Yukon named after one of the Indians, before we found trees big enough for our purpose. We worked many days cutting logs, carrying them down to the water, and floating them to the Yukon till we had one hundred and sixty-five good sized spruce logs ranging from nine inches to fourteen inches in diameter at the butt, and none smaller than seven inches at the small end.

At the mouth of the Big Minook we tied them all together into a raft which could be towed down the Yukon. When they were securely tied Al Moulton took a seat on top, we shoved the raft from the shore out into the current, and with a small boat tied to it by a two hundred and fifty foot rope, it started down the river. The men in this boat kept pulling toward the shore on which we wished to land and they had to use their every effort to do their part of the job. Just below Knob Hill was a bend in the river which caused a whirlpool and this we must avoid. They told us one man who tried to set up a sawmill to get out logs for the people lost three thousand logs in that whirlpool, and of course we were very anxious not to lose the fruits of our hard labor.

Just before we reached the spot opposite Knob Hill it seemed as though they would never be able to keep the raft from being swept down the stream and into the whirlpool, but at last they made the shore and with all hands on the rope we got the logs safely to the land.

33

Now to get them up the hill to the site we had selected for our cabin. As one of the party had already had sufficient sample of the hard work we were up against and had taken the first boat returning from Rampart City and one man had to do the cooking, we now had only ten to do the work. It was a discouraging outlook but Moulton called us all together and made a little speech.

"Boys," he said, "I know we are not used to this kind of work but just the same we will look at these hundred and sixty-five logs and then look up the hill and keep up our courage and we shall get it done."

Logging may be hard work when one has horses to pull the loads but we could not secure one. There was only one horse in the whole city of twenty-two hundred inhabitants so we just went to work and carried them up. Remember they were no small logs. Not one was small enough for one man to carry alone and some took four men to move. For some time we didn't see how we could possibly do it but finally hit upon the plan of ropes tied at one end to the log and the other end looped around our bodies. Thus our hands were free for climbing and with one or two men at each end of the log we lifted it free from the ground and carried it up the hill, and did not get it muddy as we should have done if we had dragged it on the ground. As near as I remember it took us about three days to carry the whole lot to the top of the hill, a distance of about a quarter of a mile. Every night saw us only too glad to crawl into our sleeping bags inside our tent and sleep.

We decided to build one cabin eighteen feet by twenty-four feet for our living quarters and another sixteen feet by eighteen feet in which to keep our provisions. None of us had had any experience in building log cabins but we looked at a number in the city and learned as we worked.

The side walls of course had some space between the logs and this all had to be filled with mud and moss on the outside. The roof was covered, all but two small holes left for ventilation, with smaller logs or poles from two to three inches in diameter laid as close as possible together then covered with birch bark which we stripped from the white birches which were very plentiful there at that time. On top of the bark we laid moss and then shingled it with mud.

Even in September the ground was not thawed more than nine inches and to get the necessary mud we had to dig up what we could and then wait for the sun to thaw out some more. It never thawed deeper than nine inches even in summer. Below that the ground was frozen to bed rock, and even bed rock was frozen.

When at last the walls were finished we arranged for sleeping by building bunks along the side of one wall. They were arranged like berths on board ship, one over another. For each berth we laid small poles close together as for the roof and over them we spread spruce boughs (from which the needles soon fell and left only sticks) and over these we placed our sleeping bags.

The question of where each one should sleep was an important one which we could only settle by drawing lots. Of course the top bunks were much warmer and much to be desired by all. I was the last one to draw and drew a bottom bunk in a corner where I felt the cold very acutely on many a night. Then we set up our two Yukon stoves running the stovepipe through the roof.

By this time we made up our minds we could not do without any floor so we had to find some way to saw out boards. We found some trees about a half a mile away big enough for making boards so we went out there and because we must have boards we found a way to make them. We built an open platform about six feet high and about eight feet long. Up to this on one side we erected skids on which to raise the logs into place on top of the platform. Then after measuring and drawing chalk lines on both sides we placed the log with one set of lines on top and one set on the bottom and with one man on top and one man underneath we cut out our boards with a splitting saw. Freeman was sawing underneath and I was on top and at first our boards came out about the shape of the waves of the ocean, but we soon learned to pull evenly with both hands and could make as straight a board as the best saw mills could make. Al Moulton one day called out some remark about what an easy time Freeman was having, so Freeman told him to come and try it. I had quite a task to keep the saw going while he was on the other end and I noticed he did not care to keep it up very long.

However Freeman and I worked together fine after a little while and soon had enough boards to partly cover our floor, make a table and two doors.

We stored our provisions in the smaller cabin which we always called the "shack." We had enough for two years and they had been wisely chosen so that we had all we needed to do with. Plenty of beans, good bacon, fine flour, canned milk and all kinds of dried fruit.

CHAPTER VIII

Hunting a Claim.

Now we had a home. But this was only our city home and sort of headquarters. We did not stay here all the time but only between trips and when in need of provisions. It seemed as though it was about time somebody was earning something and a number of us set out to look over some ground which had been staked out by an acquaintance and which had yielded quite a little gold the year before.

Bagley was on this trip and it being only the first week in October and not seeming so very cold he could not be persuaded to wear any mittens. We had not gone far before he wished he had them for it seemed to grow colder. After feeling the cold for some time he was only too glad to pick up a pair of gloves lying on the trail dropped there by some passerby. He immediately put them on. A little further on we saw what looked like another pair of gloves in the trail ahead, but a man coming from the other direction reached them first and when we met he had them in his hand.

"Have any of you fellows a pin?" he asked.

"Why, what do you want of a pin?"

"Why pin these together and hang them up on a tree. The poor cuss that lost them will be

37

coming back this way and he will be glad enough to find them."

"Won't somebody steal them?" inquired Bagley.

"Steal them! We hang men for stealing out here."

Bagley felt pretty small as he thought of the gloves on his hands.

What the man said certainly gave the right impression. There was almost no stealing there. The only case I ever heard of was a colored man who stole a ham. A miners' jury was called and he was tried. He had plenty of food and could give no reason for stealing the ham. The jury voted to give him twenty-two lashes. That meant more disgrace than anything else for they did not remove the clothing and the hurt was nothing very serious. However the soldiers who had recently been sent there would not allow it and said they would hold him till spring and then give him a trial at Sitka, at that time the government seat. All winter they kept him as their servant and then they let him go without any trial at all.

The miners' trials were really very wisely conducted. There was one case of three men working a claim together. They got into a scrap, used axes and guns without doing any particular harm, and the miners' jury decided to send the whole three of them away.

We visited Idaho Bar with some thought of taking a lay on the claim there but we did not like the looks very well and decided to go on. While looking around Idaho Bar we ran across a man working all by himself. He had dug a hole about fourteen feet across and twenty feet deep. Instead of making fires to thaw out the ground as most miners did he would dig down as far as he could then leave it for the sun to thaw it some more and the next day he would be able to scrape out a few inches more. In this way he had taken all summer to dig this hole but had so far run across no prospects.

This man told us about a rather disappointing experience he had been through the previous spring. He had a claim in Dawson on which he had begun to find prospects when some sharpers managed to get him drunk and bought it from him for five hundred dollars. That season they took out over a million dollars from that one claim.

One had always to be on the watch for sharpers. I heard of another man in Dawson. He was a Vermonter and knew nothing about mining but they did not quite fool him. In Dawson, which was Canadian territory, in order to work a claim one had to get a permit from the government agent for thirty days and if he wished to keep it longer he could renew it for another thirty days. If anything was taken out a certain percent was given to the government. This man had dug all alone for sometime when some fellows came along and asked if he would sell for fifty dollars. Said they had heard he was most out of provisions and would take the claim off his hands if he could not keep on.

"No, I'll dig till my last bite is gone anyway." So they had to go away. But soon they came again and offered him one hundred and fifty dollars which he refused. But he began to think there was something queer about the way his claim was increasing in value. So he went to the agent's office and told him about it.

"Have you washed any?" inquired the agent.

"Why no I have not," he owned.

The agent saw that he knew nothing about mining and advised him to get a partner. "Give him half interest and work together," he advised. The man took his advice, and as soon as the partner had washed one pan of dirt he knew that his dump was full of valuable pay dirt and together that summer they took out over a million dollars worth of gold. Then the Vermonter sold out his share, keeping certain royalties for himself and returned to his native state to enjoy his wealth.

From Idaho Bar we returned to the Tanana Trail, spent the night in an abandoned cabin, then followed the trail about fifteen miles further on to Quail Creek. Here we looked again, and the friend I have previously spoken of showed us where two thousand dollars had been taken out the year before and where he thought would be the best paying place for us to start in.

The president called together the seven of our party who were there and we decided to leave four men to work this lay. We signed a contract with the owner of the claim to the effect that twenty-five per cent of what we found was to be his and seventy-five per cent ours, and we were to have it all ready and washed out by the Fourth of July. After this was decided Al Moulton came to me and wanted to know if I would stay there and work that claim. When I said I would he told me to pick my other three men, insisting that I ought to be the one to pick my own helpers. So I chose Freeman, Mann and another man by the name of Moulton whom we called "old man Moulton."

CHAPTER IX.

The Claim on Quail Creek.

With this settled the next thing was to get
plenty of provisions for us. It was twenty-five
miles back to our city home and it took three days
to make the trip and return. A man could go in
one day if he had nothing to carry but it took two
days with a pack, so our men always went the
whole distance one day and loaded up and came
back to the old abandoned cabin about half way
between the next day, and then the rest of the way
the third day. Old man Moulton and I being the
oldest, stayed to start building a cabin while
Freeman and Mann took the trail back home for
supplies.

We found building a cabin a little different
proposition than before. This time we had the
trees all handy so there was no carrying to be
done. However, all we had for tools were an axe,
crosscut saw, hand saw, hatchet, hammer and
nails. With these we set to work to build. As
I was the youngest of the two of us I started in
to chop while old man Moulton began peeling off
birch bark to have in readiness for our roof, and
as it was now getting so cold that the moss was
freezing he gathered moss and laid it on brush
around a fire and thawed it out ready to use. I
chopped down the trees and whenever I needed

41

him he left his work to help me saw them up into the right length.

When we had quite a number of logs ready we began to lay them, following around the four sides and fitting the ends so they would lie close together. When the other two men returned in three days we had the four walls up eight feet and a few poles laid on the roof. We covered our provisions with a tarpaulin until the cabin should be ready and the men returned for more. In this way they made five trips before we had enough so we could all go to work. It was not until the last trip that we got our stove. We ate, slept and lived out of doors these fifteen days with the thermometer from twelve to fourteen below zero, but there were no storms during all this time and we were thankful for that. We tried to stay inside the cabin, but it being built out of green logs was colder than it was outside. After we got our stove up it was livable, but we had a sheet of ice down the wall behind the stove all winter although the stove stood only about a foot from the wall and was often red hot.

This might be as good a place as any to say that through all the cold and exposure and hard work and privations I never once had a sign of a cold and my health, which the doctors considered very poor when I left home, never gave me a thought while I was there and improved so quickly that I came home a perfectly well and strong man. So much I brought with me from that cold region.

I wonder if you have any idea what the miner in Alaska is up against. We took a lay of what is called gulch mining. It is on level ground. Mann and I each started a hole. To begin with we dug a hole six feet long and two and a half feet wide. We could dig down about nine inches as that was about all the sun had thawed out through the summer. Then we had to place in this hole big logs and thickly piled kindling, piling the logs into a pyramid with a large cap log on top, and light a fire at each end. Then we waited till the fire burned out, after which we would be able to dig another nine inches or less; for of course the ground is frozen solid from this point to bed rock and all digging has to be done this way. First thaw and then dig, a little at a time. When we were near the top of the hole we could make two fires a day but as the hole got deeper we could make only one. Cutting the necessary wood kept us pretty busy. The seven logs used for the fire were seven or eight inches in diameter and they would last about eleven days but we had to use lots of kindling.

After the fire burned out we took out the logs, cleaned out the hole, dug as much as we could and then relighted the fire.

People ask me why we didn't use steam. There was a party near us that did use steam and they didn't use as much wood, but we could dig two holes to their one. It was slower.

In order to cover as much territory as possible we started the second hole a little to one side and just opposite the end of the first hole and then started the third one opposite the end of the second one but back on a line with the first one, and so zigzaging in this way we dug twenty-two holes. We took about two months, sometimes all of us working and sometimes with two on the trail bringing provisions. We found colors but nothing of any value. By colors I mean little specks of gold so small it would take many of them to be as big as the head of a pin. We saved about two ounces of this gold, at this time worth eighteen dollars and seventy-five cents an ounce.

In most of these holes we struck bedrock at a depth of about fifteen feet.

One day, as each of us was digging in his

own hole, Mann let out a most exciting yell, "We have struck it, we have struck it!"

Freeman and I went over to see what he had found. And it did look good. If what we saw had been gold I should be a millionaire today. But Freeman took a knife and tried to cut some of it. The pieces flew in both directions. It was mica. If it had been gold it would have dented like lead, for pure gold is soft; but this stuff was mica which had been through fire, making it the color of gold. It was an awful disappointment to Mann.

CHAPTER X.

On the Trail and in Camp

The summer trail goes over the Big Divide which is forty-six hundred feet high and would pass for a good sized mountain here. On one of our trips over the Divide in October we climbed until we found ourselves above the clouds where only the tops of the mountains could be seen. It seemed as though there were a thousand of them. And away off over the clouds were five sundogs. It was a grand sight.

We had many experiences on the trail. Once in the middle of March I remember sitting on the sunny side of a rock eating frozen biscuits. We had carried them in our pockets and they were frozen so hard the only way we could manage to get any was to blow on one side and then gnaw at it, and then blow and breathe again till we softened up some more.

Freeman remarked, "If my wife could see me now and she didn't cry I would never speak to her again."

Toward the end of the time we spent there Freeman and Mann started on one of their trips to Rampart City for provisions. We had only enough on hand for three days for Moulton and me when they went, but the trip took three days so that did not worry us. This was the last trip they would be able to make by

the summer trail which goes over the Big Divide
for it is not safe to go over this trail in winter.
They made it all right going but on their return
Mann got frightened. Going up the Big Divide
were five steep places where one had often
to climb on hands and knees. With level places
in between it looked much like one mountain piled
on top of another. As they climbed up this place
Mann kept motioning Freeman to come back,
but Freeman who was far in the lead-motioned
back to come on. When he reached the last climb
at the top after four hours of hard work he looked
back and saw Mann going in the direction of
home. So Freeman came on alone, knowing we
were out of food in the camp.

Now Freeman was carrying a bag of flour
and Mann had all the smaller articles such as
salt, pepper, baking powder, etc. So when he
arrived we had to make bread from flour and
water with no baking powder or salt, and we had
nothing to eat with our bread. About this time
there was a bad storm which made the summer
trail out of the question any more, and as we did
not know the way by the winter trail we had to
stay there and eat our tasteless bread for
nine days. At the end of this time we had a
chance to go with a German party who knew the
way by the winter trail. It was thirty-five miles
and pretty hard travelling. I had a pack of fifty-
four pounds of stuff to take back to Rampart City
and Freeman and Moulton each had a pack. When
the party stopped for dinner we told them we
had our lunch with us. It consisted of some of
our flour and water bread which was frozen so
hard we could not bite it. So we held it to the
fire till it was black on one side and then scraped
off with our teeth what we could get. The party
we were with gave us each some hot coffee of
which they had plenty.

With my heavy pack and hard walking I got

pretty tired. The light snow covered the trail so that in one place I stepped right off into a five foot hole. It does not take many such falls to make a person feel ready to rest. So when I came to a big log that looked just right to lean against I said, "I am going to stop and rest a minute."

Freeman began to swear at me. Now I knew he was the best friend I had and I knew he didn't mean it, so I leaned there about a minute. It didn't take more than that before I began to feel sleepy and very comfortable. I was not cold or tired any more. So I thought I had better move on. As I stood up to go I fell headlong. My legs were numb and stiff, but the circulation soon started up again and I was ready to go on. I had ten miles more to go but I did not stop again, and I never was more tired in my life. It was sixty-five below zero that day and a few minutes more leaning against the log would have sufficed for me to freeze to death. That is why it is unsafe for men to travel alone in that cold climate.

We were glad to get to the cabin and although Mann must have known just what we had to eat those nine days we never said a word to him about it, for we knew the trail had been enough to turn most anyone back, and we told the others of the party that we had struck water and thought we might as well come in for a week.

Freeman, Mann and I went back to Quail Creek for about four weeks more and during this time I did the cooking. We had among our supplies a quantity of dry yeast, but up to this time we had lived on baking powder bread. My wife had taught me to make bread but I had had no experience with dry yeast. However, by using my own ideas I managed to make some good raised bread which was welcome after not having had any for so long.

We had a biscuit pan which just fitted the

oven of our little Yukon stove and which held
three loaves of bread. One Sunday I had just
made three loaves when two natives came in.
Freeman said, "What do you say, let's feed
them?"

So I fried some bacon and cut some bread for
them. They were very grateful and went away.
It was not long before two more came in and of
course I had to feed them. They thanked us and
went away and soon three more came in. One of
them was a great big man over six feet and another was a small person passing for a boy but
we all thought it was a girl. We gave her
some raisins and figs and she took off her red
handkerchief from her neck and wrapped them
up. By the time they had eaten and gone my
three loaves looked sick. I told them when they
came back from the hunt to leave us a piece of
caribou meat. They got a caribou weighing
nearly five hundred pounds but they went right
by and didn't leave us any. If a man is in trouble
of any kind a native will do what he can to help
him but if he is all right he doesn't go out of his
way to do anything for him.

One day a man called and asked if we missed
anything after our week's absence. We said we
had not.

"Well," said he, "I was passing this way and
I was tired and hungry and I looked in and saw
that your cabin was empty and you had some
bread and bacon and so I came in and cooked myself some supper. Whenever you are travelling
by my cabin come in and do the same."

One noon about the first of March as we were
at dinner a faint beam of sunshine suddenly came
through the window and we all jumped to our
feet and rushed to the window with exclamations
of joy. But before we could get there it was
gone. That was the first glimpse of the sun we
had seen all winter and it certainly was welcome.

After that it shone a little more each day, but I shall never forget the thrill that first little ray of sunshine brought us. In the far north where I was, the sun always rises in the East and sets in the east. In the long days when it is visible nearly all day it simply rises, follows the horizon around and just dips down again in the east before rising again. It never is up high in the sky as it is here in the summer.

CHAPTER XI.

Josephine Bar and Idaho Bar

By this time the twenty-two holes convinced us there was nothing there so we carried all the stuff back to Rampart City and left our cabin. At the big cabin we found only old man Moulton, the others having gone out in two parties, one on Idaho Bar and the other on Josephine Bar. Mann went to Josephine Bar and Freeman to Idaho Bar where Al Moulton was in charge. I had a chance to chop wood for a man at Rampart City so I went to work for him and old man Moulton and I occupied the big cabin alone. I had to walk five miles across the Yukon to the place where I was to chop and the first day the first stroke I took my axe handle broke with a snap. It was frozen and I had not thought of it. So I had to go back to the cabin and make another one. The next day I took the precaution to warm my handle before I started to chop and all was well. I received fifteen dollars a cord and I had cut about fifteen cords when we heard they wanted more help at Josephine Bar, so old man Moulton and I took our packs and started out to find the place although we had never been there.

We came to a big rise probably one hundred and fifty feet or more so steep we had to pull ourselves up by hanging on to branches and bushes.

I had managed in this way to almost reach the top when I took hold of one branch that did not hold and down I went to the bottom in less than a minute. By this time it was too late to go on so we left our packs and went back home. The next day we succeeded in finding the place, but they did not need any more men so we returned again to Rampart City.

I had been back at my wood chopping only a short time when Freeman came in from Idaho Bar where Al Moulton was in charge and urged me to go back with him. But I was rather slow about agreeing to this for I was getting discouraged and I had an idea Moulton didn't like me very well, so I thought I might keep out of trouble by staying away from him. But Freeman insisted that Moulton had said he wanted to see me as we had not met for three months, so I finally decided to go with him. Much to my surprise when I reached Idaho Bar and Al Moulton first set eyes on me he threw both arms around me and kissed me in his joy at seeing me again. All my imaginations had been false and he was truly glad to see me. We became very close friends after that.

The party here had three holes about thirty-five feet apart and about thirty-five or forty feet deep. They were now beginning to tunnel from one to another, and for two hundred feet more in different directions. I was given the job of tending one of the windlasses at the top of the shaft. It was the coldest job I had while there. Out in the open with the free sweep of the wind and the thermometer varying from fifty-eight to sixty-six below one could not stand still very long. I had to let down a man to work in the hole then haul up the unburned logs from the fire which had burned during the night. Then while he was digging I chopped kindling, and I was glad enough of this exercise for I had to be walking about swinging my arms whenever I was not doing anything else. When the man in the shaft had some dirt ready to bring up I pulled that up and when the hole was cleaned out I let down the back logs and plenty of kindling for the new fire. There would be several boxes of dirt cleaned out each time and we had to keep two boxes on hand for one could only be used three times before the dirt would become frozen on it so thickly it would not empty. I had to make a fire and turn the boxes over the fire to thaw them out and free them from the frozen mud.

About this time the party on Josephine Bar decided to give up there. They had put down two holes, one fifty-eight and the other sixty-five feet deep. In the first one they did not get through muck and they found shells way at the bottom of that hole, showing connection with the ocean at some previous time in the earth's history. So they moved their stuff into Rampart City, and while doing this Bagley froze his toe. He didn't know it was frozen until sitting at dinner he thought his toe kind of ached so took off his shoe and found it was frozen and only just beginning to thaw out. He was not able to do any more work for six weeks so he and old man Moulton stayed at the Rampart City cabin and some of the others came up to Idaho Bar to help us.

THE CABIN AT RAMPART CITY

CHAPTER XII.

Cooking.

This was the time when I went to cooking in earnest. I knew a little about cooking already and I had some surprises in mind for the party. They were about tired to death of baking powder bread and I started in to make raised bread at once. Then we had among our supplies some evaporated vegetables put up in pasteboard cartons which previous cooks had tried to use. They had poured on boiling water and tried to cook them. One mess had cooked for a day and a half and then they were not done and everybody thought we had wasted money buying them. I knew well enough that was not the way to cook them but I also knew my turn would come sooner or later and I thought I would keep still and have a surprise for them.

So I put some of them to soak in cold water one night and cooked them about fifteen minutes the next day, putting in a good quantity of extract of beef. When the men came in to dinner that day they began to sniff and wonder what smelled so good. And after they had tasted they wanted to know what it was. With nice freshly baked bread it went pretty good. Moulton had said, "If it tastes as good as it smells it is all right," and he decided it did. When I told them what it was they all asked how I ever cooked it.

"Why I used common sense. Instead of putting boiling water on it I put it to soak in cold water and it cooked in about fifteen minutes." My surprise certainly took that day.

When we were buying our supplies I had wanted to get spices and all such things but they didn't think we needed them so I was somewhat handicapped in trying to make variations. But we did have ginger and the next thing I made was ginger bread, which they thought was pretty good.

Of course bacon was at all times a main article of diet and I had from the beginning saved all the fat from the bacon, much to the wonder of the men who wondered what I was going to do with that stuff. Very soon I had enough to make some doughnuts and these were declared mighty good.

And finally I capped the climax with pies. We had plenty of dried fruits; apricots, prunes and peaches, and these made good filling for pies. As far as I remember I had no spice but ginger, but I chopped up raisins and put them in and they tasted all right.

All this cooking was done on the regulation Yukon stove thirty-three inches long, twelve inches wide and nine inches deep. What space was not taken up for the fire box was oven, and we had a biscuit pan which just fitted the oven and held just three loaves of bread.

I had a funny experience one day in bread making. I made my sponge at night and hung it up in a six quart pail over the stove for the night. Early in the morning the men came in to sharpen their picks. While heating them in the stove they put on such a fire that my sponge began to bake on the bottom. Well, I didn't know whether it would be any good or not but I gave it a tremendous stirring and made it up as usual. That night we had company to supper. There

were eleven men there in the ten by eleven cabin
when I opened the oven to see how my bread was
doing. And they said it was the biggest sight
they had seen for some time. The oven was
entirely filled with bread. It touched on all sides.
I pulled it out, and after scraping off the little
black on the side next the fire box, where there
were only two thicknesses of iron and one of
asbestos between the bread and the fire, it proved
to be extra fine bread, much praised by all.

CHAPTER XIII.

Mr. Holland's Claim, Moosepasture and the End of the Season.

About the middle of March we decided there was nothing on this claim worth staying any longer for, though we had found some prospects. Of course we always kept a pan of water in the cabin and each day brought a new pan of dirt to wash out. Some days we found nothing and others we found just enough to keep up our courage and make us feel we must be getting nearer, and so we would keep on. But nothing we had found so far was worth the labor involved in washing out the dirt from the winter's digging. If this dirt was to be washed out it must be done before the spring thaw started in. It meant building sluice boxes and dams and an endless amount of work. So all the men but Moulton and me went prospecting and we stayed on to put down a hole for a Mr. Holland, who owned a claim nearby but was too old to work it himself. He offered us very generous terms if we should find anything. We lived on at our own cabin. Moulton did the digging in the hole while I managed the windlass and the wood and did the cooking.

Mr. Moulton was a heavy man and as the hole got deeper I found it took all the muscle I had to let him down the hole and pull him up again, so we had to reduce the size of the cylinder from six inches to five inches. At first we made two fires a day but later could make only one and then had to throw down snow to make steam to get the gases out of the hole before he went down, and his eyes were bloodshot all the time even then. We went down eighty-five feet by the last of April and it was not safe to go down any further for the sides were liable to fall in and cover him. There were risks enough to run without running unnecessary ones.

Moulton was always very particular who should let him down by the windlass and especially after hearing of an accident which happened to one of our friends during the spring. He was being let down into a forty-eight foot hole when the windlass some way got away from the man who was handling it and he dropped to the bottom. The force was so great that the foot on which he was standing in the rope was broken so that the ankle bones protruded on both sides and he did no more work that season. The man at the windlass did not seem to know how it happened but he always had a great habit of wiping his nose with the back of his mitten and we all thought he very likely let go with one hand to do so at this time and lost control of the windlass. His mitten was found twenty-five feet away.

There was also great danger from pebbles or anything falling down the hole when the man was down there. A pebble falling down a hole eighty-five feet deep would have the force of a bullet shot from a gun and Moulton always kept something over his head when the bucket was being lowered or raised, and we at the top had to be very careful about knocking anything down.

In the meantime some of the men who had been prospecting had put down a hole on Moose-pasture. They had gone thirteen feet and said

they struck bed rock. But Freeman didn't believe
it was bedrock and he built a fire on it to see
what would happen. When he took out the fire
it was all cracked and broken up so he could take
it out in pieces and we went down sixty-two feet
more through this strange cement like formation
and didn't strike bedrock then. We were just
down to dirt again and this dirt was full of small
polished pebbles which looked as though they had
been in a river for years. In fact it looked just
like a river bottom. But one night a piece of the
hard formation above which we estimated to
weigh five hundred pounds, broke off and fell
down the hole. If a man had been down there
he would have been crushed to death, and we did
not dare to go down again.

Freeman did his best to persuade me to stay
over till another fall and then we would begin
early in the season and work that hole and see
what there was there. But I simply could not
stay another year. I had left a wife and small
daughter at home and I must get back to them.
We all went in to Rampart City to the big cabin
on the Yukon, just managing to get all our stuff
in on sleds before the snow went, otherwise we
should have had to carry it all in on our backs.

Now we had a little more leisure but as some
of the party were going to stay another year we
built a new cabin, better than the other, peeling
all the logs and making it very nice. We chopped
a lot of wood for them and got it in for the next
year. We had a chance to cut some logs and
earn two thousand dollars, but the party could
not agree on taking the job, so we did not do it.

The only unusual happening until the Yukon
broke up was a sort of field day which the Indians
or natives held on the Yukon. They played some
kind of a game with a big ball and had a big time
all day. There were between five and six
hundred there.

The twenty-second of May the Yukon broke up and it was a grand sight. The ice was anywhere from five to six or seven feet thick and when the water coming down from above and from the mountains around got under the ice there was a sound as of the booming of many cannons. The ice formed a dam below us so that the water rose fifty-five feet that night right in front of our cabin, but it did not reach to where we were. One large cake thirty-five feet wide and probably seventy-five feet high was left standing on end in front of a man's store. It had to be blown up by dynamite for fear when it melted it might fall over on someone. A man who had been there twenty-four years said he had never known the Yukon to vary more than three days in its time for breaking up. He had known it to break up the twentieth, the twenty-first, and the twenty-second, but he had never known it to vary more than that.

CHAPTER XIV.

One Thousand Miles in a Small Boat.

Now we could begin to think of starting home. Al Moulton and five others were going to stay but as for the rest of us the quicker we could get started the better we were suited. There was a man who had a small schooner who would carry men down to St. Michael for twenty-five dollars if they boarded themselves. I had partly made a trade with him when I had another proposition offered. Mr. Mills, the man who had the drop in the shaft and broke his ankle, and was still on crutches ,had a small flat bottomed boat, eighteen feet long and three feet beam, and he wanted to know if I would not go down with him. So old man Moulton and I agreed to go with him as soon as the ice was cleared out enough to be safe. We talked with the old settlers and they thought by the fifth of June it would be safe, and of course the whole town knew we were going to start with this small boat on the thousand mile trip down the Yukon with all our luggage. When mine was weighted later it proved to amount to two hundred and twenty pounds and with that of the other men and our own weight the boat settled down into the water until there was only about four and one half inches from the water line to the edge of the boat.

Everybody was there to see us start. The

Yukon is anywhere from four to twenty-five miles wide in different places. In some places it is calm and in some others it is just like the ocean with monstrous waves. We had thought we could drift with the current, but it was not safe to get into the current.

It was the fifth of June when we finally felt sure the ice would be out of the river and made our start. It was a beautiful morning when we got under way about ten o'clock but in a half an hour it was raining hard and the wind began to blow. We had to keep close to the shore and had to row all the time. Where we were at this time the sun was visible about eighteen hours out of every twenty-four and it was daylight all the time. The first night the other men lay down for about six hours while I rowed alone. I had to keep close to the shore and be on my guard all the time to keep us right side up, as we were so heavily loaded. It was a lonesome night as I thought of those at home and wondered if I should ever reach there.

The next day we came to a place where the river took a turn to the left. We were following along the right shore and as it was about five or six miles across the river at this point we thought we could save considerable by cutting across the corner, instead of keeping with the shore. It was calm, and we tried it. But just as we got about half way across, the wind came up, and how it did blow! It kept us busy heading waves so as not to be swamped and we did not land just where we expected to. But we managed to get back to the right hand shore and around the curve after a struggle.

When we left Rampart City they told us to keep to the right side of the river. The Yukon is full of small branches, which they call slues, and in following the shore one is apt to get into one of these instead of keeping on the main river and perhaps get off the course before he discovers it. All the slues leading off from the right side, they assured us, would lead us back to the Yukon sooner or later, if we should get into any of them. But if we should get into any on the left they would take us off into Bering Sea. So for this reason we tried to keep to the right all the way.

As I had not had any rest for some time and everything seemed quiet I thought, after we got around the curve, I would lie down for a little sleep and let the other two look after the boat. I don't know how long I slept, but they woke me up in a hurry for my help. There had been a shower (we often had several in a day, but not severe ones) and then the wind had risen and now we were nearing one of the slues we had heard about. At this point the main river followed the left shore while the right shore where we were led off into the branch river. The point of land in between curved around in such a manner as to cause a regular whirlpool where the water came down from above and struck against it. We didn't like to get into this whirlpool and remembering what the men had told us we decided to take the slue, for we should probably come back into the Yukon a little further down.

We did, but it took twenty-six hours hard rowing and then we had made five miles. We estimated we had traveled nearly one hundred miles in and out among the mountains. It was worse than the detours one finds in the main roads of today. We were working hard and going one hundred miles to make five. It made us rather discouraged, but the water was fine and the river also and we got in one whole day's travel without special event.

Then we struck a shower. At first it rained on shore, but in a little while we went into it, and it rained on the water but not on the shore, and we got wet. Then we came to another slue.

And this time the whirlpool was worse than before and spray flew in all directions. We didn't know what to do, but Mills said, "Don't go there; go to the right." So to the right we went. The mouth of this slue was a half mile wide and it was a pretty good sized river.

We saw a man on the shore at this lonely place and asked him where he was going.

"Going to H—," was his reply, and it didn't encourage us greatly. We asked him if he had any folks at home, and he said he had a wife, but the last letter she wrote him she told him not to come home until he struck it. We also asked him if he had heard or seen anything of the small schooner I had intended to come down on. He told us she had gone all to pieces in the middle of the river, near where we were. Said he saw her just break up all of a sudden without any apparent cause and the men swim around in the water a while and then go down. We could see some of the wreckage at a little distance. So we went on, thinking we might be worse off after all.

As we went into this slue we found ourselves facing a big snowcapped mountain and the river was so crooked and winding that we found ourselves facing this same mountain three times in the next three days. For it took us three days this time to get back into the Yukon. And we had made about twenty-five miles on our journey.

During all that time we rowed by shores that were perpendicular. Sometimes of rock and sometimes dirt, but always perpendicular. No place could we land. We came to one quiet bay we had to cross. We thought it looked about four miles across, but it took us over four hours to reach the other side, and the natives there told us it was between nineteen and twenty miles. They also said it was at times a very wild and treacherous piece of water, but when we crossed it was still as a mirror.

In this native camp so far from all civilization we were surprised to see a white woman. She was tall and good looking and we thought we would speak to her and see if there was anything we could do for her. But she would make no answer to our questions and showed no interest. We could even take her hand and she would not resist, but seemed to be perfectly passive. We could not solve the mystery of her presence there, where there was no other white person, and with her mind apparently a blank. We thought she must have been abandoned there by some white man and that her situation had driven her insane.

We were glad of the chance here to get some meat, as we had not been good enough shots to get any ducks or geese as we had planned. So we bought a red salmon from a native. It measured a little over three feet in length and we paid him two quarts of flour for it. He took his bandanna handkerchief from his neck and spread it out for us to put the flour in and picking it up by the corners, went off well pleased with his bargain.

After making a good supper from half this fish I remarked to the others that I was going to row all night. I was really the only able bodied man there. Mills was still disabled from his broken foot and could only handle the rudder, and old man Moulton was not very strong for rowing. The night that followed was one of the hardest of my experience. We were following absolutely perpendicular shores and all along next the shore was driftwood. The wind which usually had blown up stream, now changed to an oblique direction and it took all the strength I possessed to keep the boat off the driftwood. I had to pull for the center all the time and Mills helped all he could with the rudder. We expected any minute to be smashed to pieces and if we had been, we could not have gotten ashore. After two hours and fifteen minutes of this harrowing experience we found a small cove and we went in and tied up our boat. It was the first chance we had had for a good sleep and Mills and I lay right down in the boat and slept, while Moulton went on shore and made a fire and slept by that.

Sometime in the night I heard, away off to the right, a whistle that sounded like a river boat whistle. In the morning I took a walk through the woods and after about four miles of tramping came to another river, which I was told was the Andreafski and a tributary of the Yukon.

We stayed another day and night in our cove before we dared to go out on the river again. By this time the wind was again blowing up stream. We went about two miles, when we came to the mouth of the Andreafski and I told the others I had rowed against the wind as long as I wanted to. Now I had found a river that went with the wind and I was going to take it wherever it went. So we went up the Andreafski River. And up there about four miles we found the very river boat whose whistle I had heard a few nights before. I went on shore and inquired for the captain. He was pointed out to me and I asked him what he would take three men, their baggade and boat down to St. Michael for.

"Five dollars apiece and board yourselves," was his answer. I jumped at the chance. "Come around about five o'clock and the boys will help you on board," he said. I want back and told the boys we must eat a good meal as we should have no chance to get anything more for thirty-six hours. We had one hundred and thirty-five miles more to go. So we cooked the rest of the salmon and ate as much as we could. About five o'clock they helped us aboard. Mills and I found a small boat covered with canvas up on the upper deck and in this we spread our blankets and had a good sleep.

The first thing we heard the next morning was when someone called out, "Come on, you boys, wake up ,if you want any breakfast." Another voice said, "Oh, they are going to board themselves." About half past ten we got up and washed. At dinner time they all formed in line and we stood with the rest and marched in to dinner. They had a grand good dinner. I had the first piece of fresh meat I had tasted for over a year. We amused ourselves till supper time and then went to supper. We expected to pay extra for the meals, but nothing was ever said about it.

As soon as we got in to St.Michael they helped us off with our boat and we rowed ashore, just twenty-one days' after we left Rampart City.

CHAPTER XV.

St. Michael and Back to the States.

It was beginning to look like rain and we needed stakes to set up our tent, but as there were no trees at all near St. Michael, wood was a hard article to get. It took a little persistence to get what we needed that time. I went into the A. C. Co.'s office and told them what I wanted. I was sent to the master mechanic. After hunting for some time, I discovered he had gone to Nome. When I returned to the office with this information I was met with a frown and the answer that they could do nothing for me. I went back to the yard and seeing some stuff lying on the ground I picked up what I thought we needed and went back into the office. I found a worse frown than ever but I told him I had picked up some stuff and if he would come out and tell me what it was worth I would pay for it. He tried to look cross still, but he finally had to give it up and he laughed right out and said to his clerk, "Go out and see what he has." When he looked at it he told me to go on with it. So at last we had our tent stakes and they didn't cost us anything.

There were two hotels in St. Michael, each with three hundred rooms. One belonged to the A. C. Co. and the other to the N. A. T. Co. We were on the grounds of the former. As it would be about a week before we could get a boat for

San Francisco we went to a planing mill and got plenty of the shavings and made us good beds.

We had just got nicely settled when the flap was pulled open and a voice said, "Have you got room here to keep a couple of fellows?" And then as he saw who it was, "Stacey, is that you?"

It was a fellow who had gone out with us on the Laurador but had gone a different way after reaching St. Michael. Of course we were glad to meet and he and his friend stayed with us all night.

On the Fourth of July, while all the bells were ringing, we left on the "Portland" for San Francisco. We enjoyed our fourteen days on this boat very much. The captain was a Swede and a very friendly man. He had a private library out of which he would lend books to the passengers for a deposit of a dollar and a half, which was returned after the last book was returned.

We took advantage of one of the numerous offers to take us to a hotel as soon as we landed at San Francisco and after reaching our room decided our most immediate need was a bath, as we had not had a good chance to take one since leaving Rampart City. We put on our better clothes and went to a barber shop where we got a haircut, shave and bath. Coming back to the hotel we asked for the keys for a certain room. The girl looked at me and said, "That room is let."

"Yes, I know it is," I said.

Then she looked again and finally said, "Why, is it you?"

And we had a good laugh. The loss of a year's beard and a general cleaning up had made quite a change in our appearance.

We spent four days looking about San Francisco and four and a half days later landed in Chicago, where I visited friends for another four days.

Only a short journey remained between me and home, and one night I walked in to find my dear wife watching for me, and my little girl, who had not wanted to go to bed for fear of not seeing Papa when he came, was soon in my arms.

And many times as I have told this story, I have heard the comment, "What hardships and deprivations men will go through for the faint hope of finding gold!"

THE END.